Masquerade

Love, Loss and all the Dross

Masquerade

Love, Loss and all the Dross

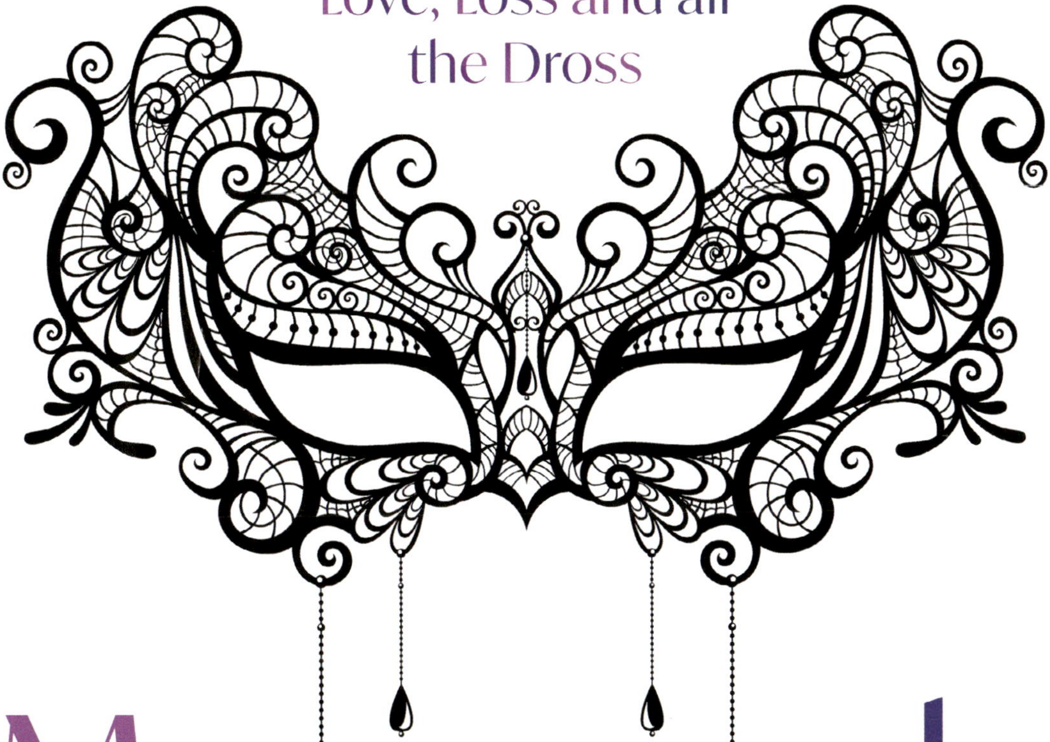

GLORIA BRADLEY

Copyright © 2024 Gloria Bradley

The moral right of the author has been asserted.

Apart from any fair dealing for the purposes of research or private study, or criticism or review, as permitted under the Copyright, Designs and Patents Act 1988, this publication may only be reproduced, stored or transmitted, in any form or by any means, with the prior permission in writing of the publishers, or in the case of reprographic reproduction in accordance with the terms of licences issued by the Copyright Licensing Agency. Enquiries concerning reproduction outside those terms should be sent to the publishers.

This is a work of fiction. Names, characters, businesses, places, events and incidents are either the products of the author's imagination or used in a fictitious manner. Any resemblance to actual persons, living or dead, or actual events is purely coincidental.

Matador
Unit E2 Airfield Business Park,
Harrison Road, Market Harborough,
Leicestershire. LE16 7UL
Tel: 0116 2792299
Email: books@troubador.co.uk
Web: www.troubador.co.uk/matador
Twitter: @matadorbooks

ISBN 978 1805144 182

British Library Cataloguing in Publication Data.
A catalogue record for this book is available from the British Library.

Printed and bound in Great Britain by 4edge Limited
Typeset in 12pt Minion Pro by Troubador Publishing Ltd, Leicester, UK

Matador is an imprint of Troubador Publishing Ltd

My heartfelt thanks to all those wonderful people who listened to my endless readings and gave me the courage to write – especially "The One".
You know who you are.

Contents

1.	Masquerade	1
2.	Creator	2
3.	Traits	3
4.	Ego	4
5.	War Lord	5
6.	Deceiver	6
7.	Journey	7
8.	Pawn	8
9.	Prayer	9
10.	Knowing	10
11.	Awake	11
12.	Gift	12
13.	Endless	13
14.	Stay	14
15.	Captured	15
16.	Woman	16
17.	Powerless	17
18.	The Dance	18
19.	Moves	19
20.	Fallen	20
21.	Miss Guided and Mr Right	21
22.	User	22
23.	Mr Nemesis	23
24.	Perfect	24
25.	Cry	25
26.	Healer	26
27.	A Moment in Time	27
28.	IceMaiden	28
29.	Contrast	29
30.	Echoes	30
31.	Steps	31
32.	Wounded	32
33.	Goodbye	33
34.	Stolen	34
35.	Incantation	35
36.	Word	36
37.	Creation	37
38.	Driven	38
39.	Only You	39
40.	Destiny	40
41.	Borders	41
42.	Blessed	42
43.	Mantra	43
44.	Unrequited	44
45.	Too Much…	45
46.	Begin	46
47.	Nirvana	47
48.	Sword	48
49.	Doorway	49
50.	Dreamer	50
51.	Fantasy	51
52.	Soulless	52

53.	Mindset	53	82.	Platform	82
54.	Peace	54	83.	Cocoon	83
55.	Lesson	55	84.	Keeping Up…	84
56.	Passing	56	85.	M'Lady	85
57.	Heaven	57	86.	Detritus	86
58.	Bereft	58	87.	Bananas	88
59.	Perhaps	59	88.	Fruit Fly	89
60.	More	60	89.	Vegan	90
61.	Starlit	61	90.	Dreamtime	91
62.	The Voice	62	91.	Alone	92
63.	She	63	92.	Signs	93
64.	Hello	64	93.	Closer	94
65.	Hidden	65	94.	You Never…	95
66.	Oblivion	66	95.	Constant	96
67.	Whispers	67	96.	Aching	97
68.	The Mist	68	97.	Mr Smith	98
69.	Wasted	69	98.	Unawares	99
70.	Gateway	70	99.	Time	100
71.	Illusion	71	100.	Pride	101
72.	Written	72	101.	It's Not…	102
73.	Dreamers	73	102.	Shallow	103
74.	Crescendo	74	103.	Mistaken	104
75.	Queen	75	104.	Encounter	105
76.	Woke	76	105.	Power	106
77.	Tattoo	77	106.	Before Too Late…	107
78.	Fake	78	107.	Three Little Words…	108
79.	Eden	79	108.	Dust	109
80.	Pinky	80	109.	Apart	110
81.	Temptation	81	110.	Broken	111

111.	Truce	112	140.	If...	142
112.	Silence	113	141.	Words	143
113.	Chancer	114	142.	Locked	144
114.	Today	115	143.	Possessed	145
115.	Distracted	116	144.	Found	146
116.	Torn	117	145.	Flight	147
117.	Adrift	118	146.	Reborn	148
118.	Light	119	147.	Moonlight	149
119.	Perfection	120	148.	One Word...	150
120.	Summer	121	149.	Surrender	151
121.	Wonder	122	150.	Elusive	152
122.	Imagine	123	151.	Mr Wonderful	153
123.	Spectre	124	152.	Diamond	154
124.	Soul	125	153.	Aura	155
125.	Lifetime	126	154.	Heat	156
126.	Ignited	127	155.	Miracle	157
127.	Unleashed	128	156.	Drumbeat	158
128.	Happiness	129	157.	One Day, One Man...	159
129.	A Fairy Tale	130	158.	Him	160
130.	Once...	132	159.	Consumed	161
131.	Empty	133	160.	Boxed	162
132.	Tempest	134	161.	Icon	163
133.	The Wait	135	162.	So Near...	164
134.	Affinity	136	163.	Portal	165
135.	Game	137	164.	Ravaged	166
136.	Eternal	138	165.	Someone	167
137.	Carousel	139	166.	Rhapsody	168
138.	Too Late	140	167.	Honey Pot	169
139.	Wasteland	141	168.	Raw	170

Masquerade

We're dancing in a Masquerade,
theatre for the masses,
each of us a player
with a script to be enacted.

Make believe, the mask we wear,
hides us out of sight,
conceals our true reality
– of power borne of light.

One day perhaps,
the mask may slip,
reveal the inner you,
awakened to an ecstasy
awaiting just for you.

So dance me to the music,
in the rhythm of your mind,
gaze my soul,
why don't you?
– in a Masquerade of time.

Creator

Is man a simulation,
processed from afar,
a thought form,
then a being,
from a galaxy of stars?

Or is there a Master Maker,
a human generator,
above the sun, the moon and stars,
creating man for Mother Earth?

Imagine we are puppets,
dangled from a string,
according to the wishes
of a God Creator King.

Woman, was created too,
fashioned from a rib,
was tempted by an evil snake
to steal an apple for her mate.

If she had been created first,
would Adam choose an apple,
or half a pint of lager,
or a burger from Macdonald's?

The tone of this short missive,
was never meant to mock,
whilst only trying hard to find,
an answer – not to shock.

The Puppeteer Creator,
Maker of mankind,
will kindly understand, I'm sure,
a little joke of mine.

Forgiveness is his speciality,
when man is led astray,
when falling to temptation,
(a woman's fault they say).

A messenger, who preached of love,
the son of our Creator,
was sent to us, an envoy,
who was to be our Saviour.

In vain he tried to make us see
the error of our ways, but in the end ,
the son and heir
was cast aside,
– and crucified.

Will man or woman never learn,
that peace and love is all,

– or, did the Lord Creator,
create a fatal flaw?

Traits

The heavens and the oceans,
the sun, the moon and stars,
Earth in all her glory,
underneath the stars…
is where
us global entities, communities of spirit,
congregate this earthly plain,
driven by dissent.

Divided by a culture or political persuasion,
racial or religious, or social persecution.

We're here to learn, to love, not hate,
learn a sacred lesson,
learn that love is all there is
– that hate is an affliction.

Forgiveness is the answer
for all our indiscretions,
– that human trait, temptation,
from which to learn a lesson.

One day, perhaps, our planet Earth,
will host humanity,
purified in spirit,
– including you and me.

Ego

Listen to the silence
of a vacant, cheerless mind,
of empty dreams, of suffering,
a soul that just survives.

Humanity is more than mind,
it's ego borne of flesh,
in worldliness, that manifests,
a lucid state of consciousness.

A gift that is the silence,
– the stilling of the mind,
tho' a heartbeat is a healer
when man is misaligned.

War Lord

War Lord.
Pray for mercy – pray in vain.

With blood on your hands, you're a man without shame;
for you it's too late,
you cannot be saved,
all the angels of heaven
will dance on your grave.

Get down on your knees,
plead for your soul,
though God will not answer
a demon of old.

The tears of the world
won't smother the flames,
when you burn in your hell,
now you've played the end game.

Deceiver

You crossed yourself for the world to see,
as though a believer,
You, the Deceiver.

You,
the Deceiver,
a loser,
a leader,
crossing yourself
in the name of the Saviour.

You're sick in the soul,
damaged, insane,
poisoned with hate
with nothing
to gain.

You cannot escape
from terror and hate,
for God in his heaven
will decide on your fate.

Birth gave you choices
for good over evil,
yours was a pact
with a black hearted demon.

Journey

We come to the planet
from realms out of sight,
born from the darkness,
into the light.

Alone on a pathway
with choices to make,
each one of us learns
from another's mistake.

It's easy to stumble
without a life plan,
when forces of evil – or good
make demands.

With love for each other,
with your hand in mine,
we'll seek the right pathway,
to find the divine.

Pawn

He went to war – then loved her more,
said goodbye for now,
a man of time and of an age,
a pawn in bloody war.

An ache subsumed her body, soul and mind,
nothing can erase it, unless he's by her side.

She's in the void where lovers go
when they are forced to part,
she's incomplete, a whisper
that pervades her breaking heart.

He went to war, she loved him more,
he said goodbye for now,
her man of time and of an age,
a pawn in bloody war.

Prayer

What puzzles me about this life
is what we're meant to be,
for good – or not,
it seems to me,
– or maybe,
wait and see…

How come that all the nations
can never quite agree,
when all we need is
peace and love,
hope for you and me?

Hope, the gift of sanity,
expressed in prayer and song,
might, through human entities,
set right so many wrongs.

My prayer for you is joyfulness,
to celebrate your birth,
created in the heavens,
– a chance to prove your worth.

Knowing

For just one moment, time stood still,
she knew it then,
she knows it still,
she needs you more,
– against her will.

She never wanted anyone,
her life was quite complete,
but when she held you in her arms,
she understood defeat.

Awake

Once, asleep from care,
– next, awake, a love affair.
Two minds transfixed, forever smitten,
though love like theirs is unforgiven.

One look is all it takes,
one touch, to light the fire,
perhaps one day that may be you,
aflame with deep desire.

Emotion is the master
or mistress of the soul,
a firelight inside one's self,
yearning to be whole.

We cannot live without it,
though it causes pain and grief,
arriving in our deepest thoughts,
a mindset under siege.

Its other power is passion,
that of merging with another,
in hot pursuit of loving,
with emotion for each other.

Gift

Do you wonder why you're here
on a planet full of fear?
why we suffer, feeling pain,
losing love or feeling shame?

The secret to such suffering
is in each others arms,
where love is given freely,
a gift that has no bounds.

The gift that's in the giving
conquers fear,
that falls as tears,
comforts when
the darkness falls,
a salve that says – "I'm here".

Endless

The love thing – where to begin?
To some it's a gift, to others a sin.

It shifts through the senses,
vibrates with a fire,
cannot be tamed
of an endless desire.

Abuse it, you'll lose it,
how sad that would be
by leaving your lover
to set yourself free.

Freedom from what,
too scared to commit
to loving forever
then live with regret?

Stay

She waited in the shadows,
for who she couldn't say,
but you came to find her,
– don't ever go away.

Stay with her, play with her,
she'll always be yours,
with you in her arms,
it's you she adores.

So, kiss her slow,
take her where,
she's lost to time
– her love laid bare.

With passion spent,
she breathes you in,
her soul is sold,
– sold to him.

Captured

Draw back the veil,
welcome the light,
reveal yourself,
it's your God given right.

Who decreed that you hide,
cancelled from view,
captured and curtained,
denied to be you?

Fight for your freedom
from those that enslave,
master your gender,
learn to be brave.

You're equal to man
not less, don't you see?
Don't closet yourself
ditch the veil to be free.

Draw back the veil
welcome the light,
face up to the world,
it's your God given right.

Woman

She's a woman,
a mother,
sometimes a lover,
sometimes a friend
on whom we depend.

She's a woman in time,
losing control,
her mindset divided,
who questions her role.

Her mood won't conform,
can't fight social mores,
trapped in a world
excessively flawed.

She's a woman in time
just doing her best,
contending with life
– just like the rest.

Powerless

Powerless, she can't resist,
the power of her lover's kiss.

She answers him with longing,
surrenders to his quest,
opens to his passion,
powerless, possessed.

Powerless, she can't resist,
without him, she can't exist.

Her love is master,
she the slave,
lost to love,
a love she craves.

Powerless, she can't resist,
the taste of him upon her lips.

The Dance

Can't eat,
can't sleep,
can't write,
can't speak.

The mind's gone soft,
the flesh is weak,
console me then,
– a kiss would do,
can't live like this
unless you do.

So, begin the dance
into the night,
make sweet music her delight.

Gently then, take your pleasure,
be fulfilled, be loved forever.

Now two are one,
the dance is done,
the music,though,
– has just begun.

Moves

Making the moves,
not making a sound,
I whisper your name,
tho' you don't whisper mine.

Let me in, your mind's locked away,
but loving's the answer,
and I am the key.

My key is a kiss
that opens a door,
leaving you free
to loving me more.

The sadness you bear
is my sadness too,
together, you'll heal
with my love for you.

This is my token of love and devotion,
I'm wanting you whole,
your heart,
with my soul.

Fallen

He invaded her senses,
messed with her mind,
she tried to resist,
but he's one of a kind.

She was mistaken,
foolish and brazen,
now she sits by a window
alone and forsaken.

Her story is ageless,
a script to be learnt,
when love is a tempter
and woman is spurned.

She'll come to her senses,
forgive and forget,
will learn from the heartache
– but live with regret.

Miss Guided and Mr Right

Miss Guided
and her Mr Right,
could not agree
and had a fight.

She lost,
he won,
her Mr. Right's
now Mr. Wrong.

User

She uses her mother,
her father,
her lover.
She's a woman,
a type,
you know what
she's like.
She couldn't care less
– her mantra at best.
Maybe she'll learn,
maybe she won't.
I couldn't care less,
who needs the stress?

Mr Nemesis

Consumed in bliss,
she met her Mr. Nemesis,
he came,
she saw,
he conquered her.

A battle raged between them,
she was never to succumb,
but her Mr. Nemesis
made sure she was undone.

Undone, but not defeated,
she claimed him as her own,
her vanquished Mr. Nemesis
had finally come home.

Perfect

She wants you out of her head,
if she hurt you, was it something she said?
What is the problem,
was it her or just you,
was she not enough,
or too much for you?
Speak to her, listen,
don't mess with her mind,
whatever has changed,
she'll understand.
How did it happen,
she thought you were fine,
was she not enough,
or too much inclined?
She knew you and her
were made for each other,
perfectly matched,
so, is it all over?

She wants you out of her head,
if she hurt you – was it something she said?

Cry

The space in my heart,
was empty and bare,
crying for help
for someone to care.
The answer that came
gave me hope and a name,
you're known as the Saviour
– a healer of shame.

Healer

Somewhere,
in the heavens,
there's a place
for broken hearts,
broken then abandoned,
– waiting in the dark.

Waiting for the one to come,
bringer of the light,
Healer of the universe,
Father of the night.

He roams the skies,
hears the sighs,
saves a soul or two,
but most of all,
the Healer,
will hear a prayer from you.

A Moment in Time

A moment in time is all we can ask,
a moment of wonder, a moment to last.

Such moments of life we savour forever,
a gift to the senses, safe and unfettered.

Hope was a gift, recalled with a sigh,
when dreams were deluded,
when you said goodbye.

As you look back in time
and remember sweet sorrow,
your moment in time,
will turn to tomorrow.

IceMaiden

A maiden of ice, a woman you know
wanders her world searching for you.

Bereft and alone, bitter and cold
with a heart of pure passion,
and love that's on hold.

Waiting for fire to burn in her soul,
your heat is a hunger she craves in the cold.

She'll melt in your arms, flow into your dreams,
thawed in the hands of the man of her dreams.

Contrast

Give it to me babe,
turn my night into your day,
be an angel to my devil,
be close not miles away.
Be the flip side of a coin,
be my shadow without form,
why fight with one another?
turning love into a war.
We could change ourselves forever,
melt in harmony together,
be as one;
contrasting,
everlasting,
me the lyric,
you – the song.

Echoes

She's aching and breaking,
no words can define,
the pain of a woman
when love is denied.

A love that's so tender.
A love with no bounds.
A love all consuming.
A love so profound.

Her hopes though, have flown,
for him in her heart,
the man of her dreams
from whom she must part.

She's losing all reason,
lost to the light,
calling his name
in the void of the night.

Her pleas to the night,
echo with sorrow
with her voice on the wind,
that mourns her tomorrows.

Steps

No matter how far,
no matter how near,
you're deep in her soul,
the salt of her tears.

Tears that kept falling
since when you first met,
who could believe
your lives would connect?

Why would you forget,
that fatal first step,
when Heaven stopped spinning,
when the sun never set?

But you walked away,
it wasn't to be,
she was for you
but you couldn't see.

She'll wait if you want,
to journey together,
one step at a time

– just never say never.

Wounded

We're wounded, you and I.
I wonder why?

Great love that comes
upon us all,
departs through
heartache's open door,
flies away, as if to say
another love
will come your way.

That door has closed,
no looking back,
it's time to love another,
but longing for that other time
is love that lasts forever.

Love is life's last mystery,
it comes on angel wings,
bestowed as if anointed
– can never be erased.

Goodbye

Goodbye is such a lonely word,
I much prefer "hello"
– hello is hope personified
goodbye – a sad farewell.

Farewell to hope, our dreams, and more,
an end to love, a shuttered door.

Goodbye, farewell, auf wiedersehen,
ciao, au revoir, we're done;
goodbye is all the same my love,
no matter where we're from.

Hello, though is a password,
a portal Hope designed,
a hand outstretched,
to heal, forget,
a word that says
have no regrets.

Next time you want to say goodbye,
remember love can never die,
hello is waiting there to say,
come, my love, I'm here to stay.

Stolen

You stole her soul, in just one day,
stole her heart, threw love away.

She's nothing, just a shadow,
adrift, awash with sorrow;
you stole her all,
her mindset too,
that day you met,
then let her go.

A foolish woman
some might say,
that waits for love,
that's thrown away.

But love is all there is
without its breath, we can't exist,
you know, and so do I,
that love can never say
goodbye.

Incantation

A gift of words,
a book of rhyme,
transports a notion
line by line.
They're drawn from dreams,
assigned a plot,
tho' story lines
may please or shock.
Poets have such licence,
for rhyme is just a song,
its music is a secret
when it rolls upon the tongue.

A tempo pounds upon a page,
beating through the senses,
sending subtle messages
to those that are receptive.

Word

How does a thought become
a word,
a word,
become a song,
a song, become a messenger,
a power for right or
wrong?

A melody accommodates
the singer of a song,
transports the mind
far back in time
to when the old were young.

A word, then, is a mystery,
unspoken – still a thought,
but borne upon vibrations,
it's a powerhouse,
a force.

Thoughts and words
of peace and love,
could heal our world forever,
but set to music
in a song

– that's mind and man together.

Creation

We're just a bunch of chromosomes,
cast from God knows what,
a product of a Maker,
a human generator.

The Maker, our Creator,
(yours and mine) of DNA,
a covert innovator,
I think it's safe to say.

When did we know ourselves as "us"
– a conscious entity,
awaking to reality,
aware of our mortality?

I wonder why we had to be
or where we were before,
were we assigned a pathway
so we'd meet to love once more?

Life's test can be too much to bear,
for some it starts with stress,
for them it's just hello, – goodbye,
when life departs with their first breath.

For others it's the opposite
with egos in full flow,
or leaders and their followers
destroying as they go.

Which one are you,
you have a choice,
to live with love and loss,
or suffer in self pity,
drowning in the dross?

I'm just the same as all the rest,
tho' loving you
is my big test.

Driven

What motivates a woman
when she looks upon her man,
what does she see,
that others can't?
it's hard to understand.

What fuels her fascination
with a man she cannot fathom,
who holds her life within his hands,
invades her inner sanctum?

Does she see a willing partner
or a father for her child,
or contemplate a future
– a role that's undefined?

When does she make her mind up
that he's the one for her,
or is she just contented
with a tender love affair?

The answer is a mystery,
– no man or woman knows,
until the spark between them
ignites each other's fuse.

With a fire quite concealed,
that cannot be extinguished,
our lovers feel the heat of it
when woman has consented.

Without the gift of passion,
we never could exist,
why would our man or woman
resist a state of bliss?

Only You

Only you,
no one else will do,
you're the one,
– her dream come true.

Only you,
can reach her mind,
make the moves,
feel the vibes.

Only you,
there's no one else,
you're all and more
in every sense.

Only you,
can free her soul,
let her fly,
make her whole.

Only you.

Destiny

She knew.

As sure as sunrise
at the dawning of her day,
as sure as when,
the sun sets,
when stars come out to play.

She knew you'd meet
one day in time,
just when she couldn't say,
but then you came,
just said hello,
as dawn unveiled
her perfect day.

Perfect in every way,
you are her dream
– her destiny.

Borders

Evil has no border – takes but never gives,
slaughters man and woman,
a path that's known as sin.

Evil has no border, leads mankind astray,
annihilates all innocence,
destroys man's destiny.

Evil has no border – rises in the ether,
casting rage and hatred,
– it's known as the Deceiver.

Evil has no border, lives and breathes with hate,
spreading like as a virus,
invades without debate.

Evil has no border, slithers in its haste,
departing each disaster,
with wastelands in its wake.

Fear not my friend, the antidote,
to evil is well known,
you and I are living proof
– it lives within your soul.

Soul, the centre – love's abode,
hears when man cries out,
begging for release to live,
in hope for humankind.

Hope and love – twin souls divine,
– await amongst the shadows,
guardians on borderlines,
– where love will conquer evil.

Blessed

Don't listen to the nattering,
a chattering of mind,
invasions of mixed messages,
wasting precious time.

Why waste your days with worries,
aggravations, daily tests,
instead of smelling roses
or truly feeling blessed?

A day starts with a promise,
a chance to be renewed,
a chance to speak, to make your peace,
or end a pointless feud.

One life is all we have,
one life to show we care,
one life to hold another's hand,
one life with love to share.

So live each precious moment,
the gift that was your birth,
love and laugh, feel your worth,
on this – your space,
on planet Earth.

Mantra

"Lovers of mankind unite"
my mantra for the world,
don't hide your private passions
from the power of your words.

Words of love, not hate, may change,
one child, a man or woman,
from suffering an absence
of kindness and compassion.

Love comes in many packages,
– a mother for her son,
– a father for his daughter,
or the lyrics of a song.

A song could work the magic
that speaks of love not fear;
your voice could be the answer,
heal a world that drowns in tears.

"Lovers of mankind unite"
my mantra for the world,
don't hide your private passions
from the power of your words.

Unrequited

Explain to me this
world of pain,
when man meets woman,
bears his name,
his name forever
on her lips,
the very same
he longed to kiss.

She dreams of him, a reverie,
of unrequited love,
lost to her, a memory,
when love's misunderstood.

Misunderstood, tho' not forsaken,
perhaps, one day, maybe,
life and fate together,
might bring them harmony.

Explain to me this
world of pain,
when man and woman part,
it only takes a moment
to heal a broken heart.

Too Much...

She never thought
to feel like this,
no-one for her – she didn't care
– until that day,
she saw him there.

The ache she felt
when loving him,
became too much to bear,
he seared her soul
but he grew cold,
left her mind a mess,
but still she longed
as women do,
longed for his caress.

Was she too old
or not enough,
ugly or too fat,
her body not so perfect,
or living in the past.

She never thought to feel like this,
a woman past her prime,
she loved him more
than she could say
when he became,
her yesterday.

Begin

Come lie with me,
kiss me slow,
never, ever
let me go.

Come lie with me,
let us begin,
make me your own,
skin to skin.

Come lie with me,
your heat with mine,
soul to soul,
mind to mind.

Come lie with me
for ever more,
my one and only,
true amour.

Nirvana

Take me.
Take me to Nirvana,
the gate to Paradise,
Heaven on this earthly plain
to leave me satisfied.

Take me.
Take me to Nirvana,
in your arms, enclosed with mine,
steal my soul,
my mind, my all,
leave the world behind.

Take me.
Take me to Nirvana,
promise to be mine,
dissolve me with your eyes,
your lips,
dance me with your fingertips.

Take me.
Take me to Nirvana,
dream me into time
where we can be forever
– forever intertwined.

Sword

The pen, someone said,
is mighty, a sword
– in the hand of a poet
can defeat with one word.

It cuts with a flourish
designed to attack,
despatching a message
signed with éclat.

It births in the notions
of mind – inner thoughts,
exposes emotions
releasing dark thoughts.

How mighty the sword
of a handwritten word,
charged with a mission
in prose or a clause?

In one simple stroke,
each letter defines
the laws of the land
in treaties through time.

It seals with bravura
the end of a war,
or a letter that speaks
of love,
evermore.

But,
– only three words
have such power and might,
the words of "I love you"
strike straight from the heart.

Doorway

"Act like a doormat,
get treated like one,"
words she remembered
when he was long gone.

She'd opened a door
when he said hello,
melted with wonder
– if only she'd known,
that this was the one,
she'd love evermore,
lost in the light
of him she adored.

Bathed in the light,
(from where she had hidden,
denying herself
a reason for living),
– he gave her the gift
of a moment in heaven.

But he left without warning
left her to mourn him,
left her as though
she was foolish and wanton.

"Act like a doormat,
get treated like one,"
is a mantra for lovers,
– when love is undone.

Dreamer

This is not a love song,
'cos love was not your thing,
your love was lost to someone else,
there wasn't room for me.

I knew that when you held me,
you were far away,
away in dreams of yesterday
where I could never be.

Perhaps I was that dreamer too,
a fool for love maybe,
or just too much
or not enough
for you to care for me…

This is not a love lament
but just a sad goodbye,
so thank-you for the memory,
of dreams that passed me by.

Fantasy

How can one man
dissolve her pride,
reduce her to a shadow,
suffocate her every breath
by wanting more
than she can give?

She cannot live without him,
heal the pain
she cannot hide,
he was her all,
her everything,
was he not satisfied?

Is she to blame, or was it him,
when he backed off, when asked again,
– was love for him a fantasy?

He wouldn't answer,
– couldn't say...

She lost him then,
he walked away,
her mystery man,
a fantasy.

Soulless

He was her one and only,
her stairway to the stars,
when he led her to Nirvana
through the gateway of her heart.

Her story though – as old as time,
started with a hug,
ended in a heartbeat
with a silent, soulless shrug.

Who was this man,
that came and went,
stole her soul
without consent?

Mindset

Who's the giver, who's the taker
when at war with one another,
in a world of near insanity,
divided from each other?

Who can tell, from him or her,
the good, the bad, the insincere?

Compassion, though
from me or you,
may help to change
the status quo,
a smile, a touch,
a friendly word,
is easy – doesn't cost the earth.

We're here to seek,
console, defeat,
a loneliness,
of mind,
with answers
that may heal the pain,
when hope is lost
in shattered dreams.

Peace

My body's here,
– my heart's elsewhere,
where's yours?
it's not with mine.

Did you lose it
when you lost her,
when you lost
your peace of mind?

Another peace is waiting,
tho' it's hard
for you to see,
beyond a veil
of misery,
– unless you come to me.

I can't promise to be perfect
or fill that empty space,
I can, though,
give you comfort
with the warmth
of my embrace.

My body's here,
– my heart's elsewhere,
it found its
way to yours,
two hearts that beat,
the music's sweet,
– perhaps for evermore…

Lesson

Back then, it was a woman,
the spectre of his dreams,
who haunted him with memories,
and all the in between.

His tears dissolved those memories,
washed away his pain,
life's lessons had succeeded
when he learnt to love again.

Love though never changes
from the first time we all know,
when love was pure and simple,
from which we learn to grow.

Those dreams remain, as we grow old,
perhaps they're more intense,
when man might meet a woman
with more love
– than common sense.

Passing

Will I still love you
'til the end of time,
when sun and moon
the stars above,
are shaken, then collide?

Will I still love you
when the heavens pass away,
when the darkness overcomes,
when the God's have had their way?

Will I still love you
at the dawning of an age
where sun and moon,
the stars above
decide to rearrange?

Will I still love you
when the world will be reborn,
when love will be our everything,
when you will be my own?

Will I still love you
through the passages of time,
in the portals of the Universe,
safe from humankind?

I will, if you still want me,
so I'll ask you one more time,
will you come to meet me
as my Time Lord in the sky?

Heaven

Is Heaven here, or over there,
with me or you,
or God knows where?

Is Heaven where my mind goes to,
when we're alone, just me, with you,
alone to love, be one, not two,
safe, cocooned, as lovers do?

I ask, because I think you know,
it's where you are,
when I'm with you.

Will Heaven hear
my lonely cry,
if love for you
should ever die?

I'm searching for an answer,
hidden in a mist,
a secret in some,
secret realm, beyond,
in states of bliss.

Bereft

Did he ever say goodbye?

She never heard him say;
she could only memorise
the way she felt that day.

She felt the pain inside herself,
her heartbeat told her so,
vibrating to the beat of his,
a man she hardly knew.

A man of many talents,
a man she hoped would care,
her man that came,
who walked away,
left her in despair.

She closed her eyes
– remembered him,
the man she thought she knew,
her heartbeat still vibrated,
when she hoped he'd feel it too.

It pounded with a passion,
she could hardly bear,
when she closed her eyes,
– imagined,
that he was standing there.

In time she would erase him,
find time for other loves,
– her heart tho' will remember,
the man she loved
– and lost.

Perhaps

Lately, she had loved again,
opened to her passion,
late in life, and free to be,
she found her piece of ecstasy.

His gift was her salvation,
enfolded in his arms,
Paradise incarnate,
a night amongst the stars.

Will her dream be broken,
could that moment last,
will the gates of Paradise
close and hold them fast?

She'll hope and wait for miracles,
for dreams to last forever,
to love like this eternally,
in Paradise together.

More

You're more to her,
than she can bear,
why can't you see,
or don't you care?

She'd turn the tides,
dissolve the skies,
if only you would realise,
that you and her
were meant to be,
two as one,
why can't you see?

You're more to her,
you just won't see
the power of her passion,
a power that ignites her soul,
inflames her inner sanctum.

One day perhaps – maybe your last,
is when you'll surely see,
the power and the glory
of what you meant

– to me.

Starlit

Starlight from the heavens
guided three wise men,
come to worship and adore
a son of God – the promised Lord.

The story, full of wonder,
a miracle of birth,
of a virgin then appointed,
by an angel come to earth.

A mystery is buried here
in the mists of time,
were those ancient travellers
angels from the skies?

Angels from a starship,
the one that showed the way,
come to save the nations
from a far off galaxy.

It makes more sense
than kings of men
riding on a camel,
following a starlit sky,
bearing gifts to glorify.

Could that angel be the one,
the guiding light
from up above,
who came to say,
we're here to stay,
come to earth,
on Saviour's day?

The Voice

Emotion caught her unawares,
his voice, melodic, deep,
eloquent with longing
in a song of love's defeat.

All the pain of life well lived
vibrated in the air,
a singer in the throes of love,
his mind and heart elsewhere.

The voice evoked a tenderness
attuned to love and loss,
moody, blue, revealing,
a love he found, then lost.

She closed her eyes,
absorbed each note,
his voice seduced her soul,
sent her to another place,
healed and made her whole.

His voice, at last
had healed him too,
when she returned to him,
a woman that,
had heard him sing,
– his voice had
made her love again.

She

Where do you go
in the shadows,
a darkness destroying
your mind,
where she of the past
keeps invading,
won't leave you alone
to be mine.

Open your eyes, be enlightened,
see the light that will guide you to me;
my arms will be waiting to hold you
with love to set yourself free.

Free from the shackles that bind you,
awakened if only you'd see,
that she of the past is a memory,
a shadow that keeps you from me.

Hello

Come, just say hello,
brush her lips,
whisper deep,
– a move you make
she can't resist.

Come, just say hello,
take her where
she wants to go,
– heal her ache,
don't hesitate.

Come, don't go,
just say hello,
then she'll love you
evermore,
with all she has
and then some more,
– her heart,
an ever open door.

Hidden

You've just become a memory,
tho' safe inside her heart,
where you will live forever
– together, but apart.

She thought that she would rather die
than live without you there,
her love was pure and simple,
all yours if you should dare.

But now, you're just a memory,
fading day by day,
tho' she will still be with you
when her heartstrings
start to play…..

a song of love, forsaken,
of when you turned away.

Oblivion

Oblivion – for dreamers
is where their dreams must rest,
awaiting to awaken,
from the darkness into bliss.

Oblivion – that great abyss,
of wasted love,
of nothingness,
haunts a soul with longing,
in a void of emptiness.

Oblivion – is waiting
if she never loves again,
crazed, forever wanting,
living on the edge.

It may be that, Oblivion,
will one day fade away,
in clouds of tears,
that disappear
– if she should love again.

Whispers

Ti amo, amore,
or in French, Je t'adore,
expresses a love,
of longing
for more.

The language of love,
that lovers create,
sings with a passion
of love and
heartbreak.

So whisper her softly,
ti amo, amour,
in French or Italian,
– or just,
Je t'adore !

The sound of his soul
vibrates with her own,
when he whispers her name,
she's out of
control.

Ti amo, amore,
Je t'aime, mon amour,
come, let me love you,
let me be
yours.

Ti amo, amore,
or in French, Je t'adore
words of a lover
who's longing
for more.

The Mist

They say that fate is written
in a story from the stars,
untold, as yet, awaiting,
to unfold within our hearts.

A mist of Time divides us,
unseen from human eye,
two souls await a future
when Time and gods allow.

That veil of mist must fade one day,
reveal a reason why,
the gods may have forsaken us
from planet Paradise.

If Time and man with woman
is where we're meant to be
why are we still waiting
to share our destiny?

Wasted

One step at a time
wasn't for me,
when I fell in your arms,
my soul was set free.

I took a chance,
(I think you did too),
but then I was lost,
with my heart lost to you.

Don't waste any time,
(there isn't much left),
wondering why
about something I said.

I'm drowning in dreams
with you in my head,
can't live with myself,
– I only exist.

So take just a step – or maybe another,
take me, why don't you?
then make me your lover.

Gateway

My soul is old, it's just like yours,
well travelled from afar,
a soul to soul,
awakening,
to wish upon a star.

Your star is where you'll find it,
deep within my heart,
its pulses beat a tempo
in mourning, when apart.

A galaxy of love awaits
for you and me together,
if you should find me waiting
at that Gateway, called, Forever.

So will you keep on searching
through a veil of memories,
of endless love,
of hope and dreams,
– seduced by
starlight fantasies?

Illusion

I only said, "I miss you,
– will we meet again,
it's been so long,
a month or more
– hope we haven't closed a door?"

You are my friend,
are you still mine?
to share a problem
– understand….
I'm all grown up (I've lived a bit),
– I'm under no illusion,
will we forget – or just regret,
that we were ever friends?

Never, ever, will I think of you,
without a tear or two,
because you were the world to me,
– was I the world to you?

Love is such a precious thing,
it comes without a warning,
none of us immune from it,
but worth a world of yearning.

Tomorrow is another day,
yours and mine apart,
yours to be with,
what's-her-name,
– mine,
a brand new start.

Written

A book is birthed in words
through time,
of all that might have been,
records man's fate or fortunes,
mankind has overseen.

Its power is in
the written word,
relived in pen and ink,
preserved for generations,
as a lasting testament,
– or a letter to a lover
before a bloody war,
addressed to a beloved,
unopened, – him no more.

Fortunes have been made or lost,
recording history,
in telling tales of heroes
– or those that lost their way.

A holy writ on blocks of stone
hidden in the sands,
will tell a tale
from gods and kings,
to help us understand.

Poets have this power too,
in rhyme that has two rules,
one of which, the written word,
the other is its tune.

Together they will harmonise,
at play with one another,
in messages,
a litany,
in verse – designed for lovers.

Dreamers

Heaven, they say,
is far, far away,
I know that's not true,
– when heaven's with you.

Who did the choosing,
gifting to me,
love all consuming,
– a love meant to be?

Let's journey together,
each one for the other,
all others forsaken,
– my love for the taking.

We are the dreamers,
love is the master,
embracing emotion,
– for love ever after.

Let's fly, you and I
to travel together,
unshackled, set free,
just you,
– and just me.

Crescendo

In the beginning,
safeguarding a soul,
the waters of life
vibrate in the womb.

Such waters within,
lapping a beat,
of a musical mystery
where a soul is asleep.

Are these the first moments,
when a soul must awake,
attune to the waters,
assigned a heartbeat?

Their harmony comforts,
soothes such a soul,
bathed in an ocean,
a spiritual home.

Will a soul have a memory
of the music of life,
borne in crescendo,
birthed into life?

Queen

She's born a bee,
tho' born a queen,
a role for which she's chosen,
she lives within a honey trap
of hexagons and candle wax.

Her baby bees are nurtured,
tucked inside a hive,
attended by an army
ensuring they survive.

Soon, our queen will say goodbye
when honeybees begin to fly.

Her task is done.
Her days are done.

And now she has to die.

Woke

Is it a noun?
or is it a verb?
Whatever it is,
it gets on my nerves.
Could woke be a joke,
a political poke,
aiming a barb,
to show who's in charge?
No! it isn't a joke
to sensitive folk
sick of the sound
of woke, woke, woke.
Woke's wanton crusaders
are social dictators,
dividing a nation
with verbal castration.
Don't bully me out
of my feminine world,
I'm happy as woman,
lady or girl.
You woke if you want,
have a nice day,
just leave me alone
to live my own way.

Tattoo

You've seen tattoos in silly places,
like those on folk with scribbled faces,
up the arms and down the legs,
lookalikes in blue and red.

It's fashion – I feel left out,
my skin is white and all washed out.
I had a thought, it just occurred,
I'll start a trend (I'm quite disturbed).

I thought about one just for me,
designed to match my mood,
I'm going for a WORDY one,
like those on packs of food.

I think I'll go for "SELL BY DATE",
or "BEST BEFORE " maybe,
No! that's wrong, it ought to be,
"BUY ONE GET ONE FREE" !

I've had it now for several days,
tattooed above my brow,
my earrings are two tins of beans,
I'm in demand right now!

Fake

What you see
is not really me
when I'm painted and powdered
showered and scoured
ready and waiting
to face a new day.

I'm adept at deception
when covering up
all the fat bulges
with oversize tops.

The teeth are all mine
only just 'cos they're capped,
some with gold highlights
others near black!

Next is the hair
Oh Lord! what to do?
I rely on those products
that set it like glue.

Now my face is a problem
do I powder or paint
or leave it alone
to dis - inte - grate?

But the eyebrows do test me
they're skimpy and fine,
then there are the lashes
that take too much time.

Thank God for the lipstick,
that's all I can say,
without it I'm done for
(it would ruin my day).

Now you see how I fake it
don't believe what you see,
though look in the mirror,
are you just like me?

Eden

When God created Eve, they say,
he stole a rib from Adam,
made her second class, methinks,
subordinate, a madam.

Forever in his shadow,
a temptress to the last,
though mother to his children
while he foraged in the grass.

Man today is much the same,
his woman, much like Eve,
but time has changed since Eden
– Adam's grass is more like weed.

Smoky Joe, the demon,
still lurks amongst mankind,
searching for an apple tree,
and Eve – if she's inclined.

Pinky

I'm not a pinky person,
you know the type I mean,
all pink lips, pink cheeks,
pink dress,
sickly sweet,
proper dense.

No! I'm not a pinky person,
more a denim blue,
fading round the edges,
washed out,
but sadly true.

A pinky person might agree,
her colour palate's so not me!

We might make friends
and blend our shades,
from pink to purple,
start a craze.

Or I might chance
a change and swap,
my denim jeans
for her pink frock.

But it won't work
'cos she's still dense
and I'm worn out
– it makes no sense.

Temptation

When Eve first met her Adam
at the garden gate,
she offered him an apple,
he bit it with distaste.

Alarmed at his reaction,
she tried to calm him down,
asked him what the matter was,
as he retched upon the ground.

"You tainted me – it's not a 'Cox',
I want a 'Granny Smith'!"
She smiled at him quite graciously,
– (the snake just licked his lips).

"I tell you what," Eve whispered,
"I'll cook you up a treat,
we've sinned it's true, and we must die,
but first I'll make an apple pie!"

Adam was transfixed with joy,
– (the snake was not impressed),
he slithered off this mortal coil,
we humans know the rest.

Who would know that apple pie
gave Adam his first fix?
that Eve – she was a wily one,
her custard did the trick!

Platform

Social platforms like "THE NET"
are not quite what they seem,
they're really not for standing on,
waiting for a train.

I've visited the WORLD WILD WEST
seen TITTER and the rest,
WHAT'S UP, NICK NOCK, FACELESS too,
perhaps I'm on there searching you!

I logged onto the SIN – TERNET,
was scammed along the way,
all I really wanted was,
to chat about my day.

My password, what a nightmare!
it refused to let me in,
then a message just informed me that
A HACKER'S BROKEN IN !!

Cocoon

What makes a creepy caterpillar,
spin a silk cocoon,
hidden in a crusty case,
bespoke, a living tomb?

Idyllic for the solo life,
away from nosey neighbours,
she's self contained and insular,
safe from such invaders.

Oh yes! It seems so perfect,
no mortgage or high rents,
but lazing in a bed all day
she soon outgrows her nest!

A nibble here, a nibble there,
the wormy one has woken,
crunching through the crispy crust,
demolishing her home.

A hole appears, she struggles,
keen to reach the light,
a miracle from worm to wings,
a butterfly in flight.

She makes a grand appearance,
is free to pick and choose,
a mate with whom to consummate,
freed from her cocoon.

Two butterflies in hot pursuit
are much like human folk,
cocooned away, but then one day,
they meet, then fall in love!

Their summertime won't last too long,
their eggs will soon be hatched,
their caterpillar babies,
must learn a silken craft.

Keeping Up...

Keeping up
appearances
each day is such a bore,
thinning bones and wrinkled toes,
Lord, there's SO much more.

Blue veins have surfaced
on my legs,
like A roads on a map,
– Google and the RAC,
could use them on their Apps!

Lipstick is my pleasure though,
it gives me one big fix,
creates a special ambience,
pretends I'm twenty-six.

Looking back at pictures
when I was just nineteen,
a bride and then a mother,
– my body took the strain!

Left it like a curtain,
draped around my middle,
never to return
to its original position.

There's more, oh yes there is,
I'll get this off my chest,
– that's another thing that puzzles me,
what happened to my breasts?...
I could go on and
on and on,
(perhaps you think I have),
but now you know my secrets
and all my inner passions.

It's all too much,
I've reached an age
when all of me has wilted,
– my mind though is a power house

but nobody has noticed!

M'Lady

Lady Lola is all honey,
with eyes of liquid brown,
her lashes long and languid,
a princess born refined.

She's graceful and well mannered,
as she offers me her hand,
then lays it on my shoulder
– as if to say you're mine.

Her hair, a cloud of tussled curls,
untamed by comb or brush,
Bohemian in splendour,
that crown her Lady looks.

She lays and drapes
upon her bed,
then softly turns
her sleepy head,
towards me with a dreamy gaze,
M'Lady at her rest.

A Lady, though a madam,
when she sidles up to me,
knows just what I'm thinking,
senses what's for tea..

Her appetite surprises me,
supping from a saucer,
licked her lips deliciously,
devoured all I gave her.

Exhausted with excitement
from the feast she had enjoyed,
M'Lady gazes up at me,
a Lady to her Lord.

As becoming to her status,
lying next to me,
fluttering long lashes,
she sighed, then fell asleep.

But just before she drifted off,
she offered me her paw,
as if to say, I love you,
but then began to snore.

Detritus

This is a tricky subject,
bear with me if you can,
it concerns so many of us,
so I know you'll understand.

It's about those pesky pigeons,
detritus in full flight,
depositing their cargo
on my car that's parked outside.

Right next to it, a lovely tree,
but since it grew so high,
it's perfect as a pigeon perch,
a mating paradise.

The car is old and so am I
but cleaning off the dross,
is wasting lots of water
when I can't afford the cost!

I'm short you see, can't reach the roof,
I might just topple over,
break a leg – or worse my neck,
take ages to recover.

So I went through all the channels,
the council several times,
my MP's assistant
but the Highways' man declined.

I wrote a pleading letter
to the man in Public Health
who read my mournful missive
then replied with his advice:

– said he couldn't help me
but be sure to wash your hands!

WELL!

I stuttered and I spurted,
the foam flew from my lips;
did he think I was so stupid
like the others that were thick?

Meanwhile, said detritus
rained upon my car,
great fat lumps of greeny muck
that wasn't from the stars.

So now I'm getting frazzled,
it's doing me no good
as I watch and wait,
the pigeons mate
above my car
– FOR HEAVEN'S SAKE!!

So once again,
I did complain,
this time it was a woman,
Glory be! she's just like me,
– says she'll see,
"let's hope you'll soon
be pigeon free."

Hope eternal came to pass,
one day two men arrived,
trimmed the Silver Birch outside,
left me quite surprised.

The magic only worked so long,
the birds are back in town,
perhaps I'll bake a pigeon pie,
before it gets me down!

Bananas

What happens to bananas?
'cos just the other day,
I bought some "in the green" – to last,
before they rot away.

It would be nice to eat one,
but storing them just right,
depends upon my timing
– and my random appetite.

Should I buy just one or two,
eat them straight away,
or five or six,
(just in case)
I need a daily fix?

But here they are before me,
dying as we speak,
yellowing with browny bits,
no one wants to eat.

Since my options are quite limited,
I'll pop some in the freezer,
make ice cream with lots of cream,
flavoured with vanilla!

I'm told that ripe bananas,
(not ripe but one big mess),
are great for making compost,
for the fruit flies to infest.

My refuse bin is not the place,
I can't do that – because,
the Wokey lot
would cart me off,
banana skins and all.

SO,
I've buried them to feed the plants,
(organics is my thing),
the neighbours though
will wonder why,
my Monkey Tree
is blooming!

Fruit Fly

Tell me why a fruit fly
hovers over me,
whilst sitting on the sofa
drinking cups of tea.

It's almost like a friend to me,
a lonely individual,
circling my habitat,
then landing on the table,
– from where it flies
to dive once more
to swoop upon my cake,
when I'm about to take a bite,
it floats around my face!

I take a swipe – it darts away,
I swear it has four eyes,
catch me if you can it says
before it makes a dive.

The next time,
when it lands again,
drowning in my tea,
it floats around in circles,
dead as
dead
can be!

Vegan

He said, she said, (no-one was a winner),
all she wanted was to say,
"what would you like for dinner?"

It caused him to combust with rage,
– asking stupid questions,
when all he really wanted was
a steak with Bird's Eye peas.

It sent her into spasm,
a vegan to the last,
her menu was the epitome
of veggies turned to mush.

It started with an algae shake,
then a tofu burger,
presented on a fragile plate
of Japanese rice paper.

Dessert was just an apple,
complete with stalk and pips,
(good for his digestion,
kept him "regular" and fit).

The marriage of these two, it's true,
survived (but only just),
when he agreed to swap fried eggs,
for butter beans on wholemeal bread!

This went on until one day
temptation drove him far away,
into the arms of one who could,
provide him with the food of love.

"If music be the food of love"
(Shakespeare said as much),
perhaps a plate of fish and chips
was just enough to do the trick!

Dreamtime

The Dreamtime is a mystery,
the universe won't share,
only with a sleeper
when the mind is unaware.

Are all our dreams a picture book,
with tales that intertwine,
or windows into wonderlands,
a jigsaw of the mind?

Dreamtime, like a butterfly,
flutters in full flight,
journeys through the senses,
lingers through the night,
with images that flicker
on a screen inside our heads,
drifts amidst the ether,
hovers round a bed.

Time is turned, the clocks have stopped,
showtime has begun,
a dreamer lost in fantasy,
adrift, beyond reality.

Meanwhile, the clocks begin to tick,
time has passed, time to wake,
the dreamer blinks, he's back in time,
day has dawned, the dream has died.

Spectral dreams may come and go,
as night will turn to day,
when once again, a day dream
invades a mind – again.

Alone

Do we die, for want of love,
or live, as others see,
a face, a mind, a body,
– like the woman, that was me?

She longed for love to let her go,
release her, set her free,
free from pain and passion,
– a woman, just like me.

Did you ever love her
when you held her one last time,
held her fast as though it was
a last and sad goodbye?

She felt a chill
– her heart stood still,
it died from loving you,
she's just a shell, now she's alone,
without your heart,
she's turned to stone.

Signs

Where are the signposts
guiding the way,
– the ways of the world,
steps we must take ?

We come to a crossroad,
the signs are all there,
we're just the choosers,
– with crosses to bear.

A step to the left or
right into light,
are choices to make
for most of our lives,
with love for mankind,
in brotherly love,
and all of us women,
– a proud sisterhood.

Some signs are obscured,
barred from the light,
a light that must guide us,
– turn wrongs into right.

Must we obey – someone else,
when at war,
or choose to upkeep,
the peace for us all,
– or do we obey, a leader of sin,
a son of the darkness,
by following him?

Pathways to love, tho',
are littered with tears,
signposts ignored,
when the heart disobeys,
– disobeys all the signals
directing a path,
we know that will lead us
– to love, that can't last.

Perhaps not, my friend,
no matter what,
– for love is a path
that can never be lost.

Closer

Will you let me love you
the way you want me to?

I'll wipe your tears,
soothe your fears,
make your dreams come true.

Come closer then,
let me in,
don't let me go,
let love begin.

Let me be your one and only,
kiss me angel, oh so slowly,
take my hand, guide me where
love is hiding, show you care.

Let us love, as one not two,
your soul with mine, me for you.

Let me love,the way you want,
let me be your only one.

You Never...

You never made a promise,
or said you cared at all,
always left her wondering,
or waiting for a call.

Was she just one of many,
hidden like the rest,
thinking they were special,
but really second best?

Perhaps you'll never find "the one",
(your time is running short),
but if you do,
let's hope she won't
do the same
to you.

You never made a promise,
never said you cared,
her fault perhaps – for loving you,
that left her in despair.

Love comes freely from the heart,
– hers was yours, right from the start.

Keep it safe, because you see,
you'll always be,

– a part of me.

Constant

Without you
– she is sorrow,
a mist of tears
– a shadow.

Sorrow is a price we pay,
when love decides to walk away,
all dreams dissolved,
all hope dismissed,
healed only with
– a tender kiss.

Tenderness, the key to bliss,
her pathway to the stars,
where dreams ignite
to satisfy,
– a moment in her arms.

Her love is constant,
always true,
where all will be forgiven,
without you, tho',
she's nothing.

With you, she found her heaven.

Her dream will always be of you,
the one who walked away,
who drowned her dreams,
dismissed a kiss,
that promised her,
a state of bliss.

Aching

She's aching and breaking,
dying inside, fading away,
losing her mind.

What had she felt,
the moment she saw,
the man of her dreams,
she'd come to adore?

Was there a woman,
a woman he loved,
someone like her,
who loved him too much?

Was he fake, with two faces?
one good
– and one bad,
real or not,
she longed for him back.

She asked him,
"why can't you
be mine to adore,
return all my loving,
let your soul soar?"

Adoring, demented,
with arms open wide,
she'd waited and wasted
for him by her side.

She's aching and breaking,
dying inside,
fading away
– for him to decide.

Mr Smith

Oh! Mr. Smith,
who were you?
when you wandered through my life,
who searched then found
the treasure,
of love,
I'd saved inside.

Oh! Mr. Smith,
where were you?
in the shadows of your mind,
when holding me so tenderly,
how could I be so blind?

Oh! Mr. Smith,
who were you?
when I searched your eyes with mine,
was what I saw,
a mirage,
in the mirror of my mind?

Oh! Mr. Smith,
– my Nemesis,
would you have known – or cared?
when you became that mirage
in a shroud of falling tears.

Dear Mr. Smith,
remember this,
emotion is the key,
so use it then, unlock your heart,
then give it back to me.

Unawares

He wasn't what she wanted,
when he caught her unawares,
invaded all her senses,
drove away her fears.

He changed her without trying, though,
– took her to the edge,
nothing more existed,
only him inside her head.

He roams her soul, a traveller,
underneath her skin,
mind to mind, her love entwined,
wanting all of him.

He wasn't what she wanted,
when he caught her unawares,
invaded all her senses,
drove away her tears.

Losing love is simple,
finding it not so,
takes you unawares – until,
it breaks your heart in two.

So once again,
her fears and tears
lay locked away, well hidden,
if anyone should notice
when her mind had lost all reason.

Time

Before, in time,
(when Time stood still),
we waited to awaken,
destined for each other,
from the heartlands of creation.

And so it was when destiny,
(The Fates), decreed it so,
for both of us to be as one,
to dance the dream,
as lovers do.

Too soon, our dreams
will start to fade,
Time will pass us by,
fate will once again decree,
it's time to say goodbye.

We'll meet again, just as before,
this life is short you see,
but back in Time, is where I'll find
you're waiting
– just for me.

Pride

Why her?
Why you?
Who were you two
who met one fateful day,
when all of her
– and all of you,
were one
– and meant to be?

What made you think
she was the spare,
a woman on the side,
to cast away, a throwaway,
a woman with no pride?

Her pride's intact,
is yours? – perhaps,
her fault was in believing,
when you became her everything,
– so was she only dreaming?

Why her?
Why you?
I wish I knew, because, you see ,
she still wants you.

Wants the man she understood,
his heartache and emotions,
to share the very soul of you,
– as no one else could ever do.

So was she only dreaming,
deluded with a passion,
a gift you took, discarded,
that left a broken woman?

What made you think
she was the spare,
a woman on the side,
who loved, then lost
her everything, her all
– except her pride?

It's Not...

It's not your money, home or car,
none of the above,
nor is it all those memories
of women you have loved.

It's not your goods and chattels
or books on dusty shelves,
(your music, though's a maybe),
you know she loves it so!

It's not the younger man you were,
in photos with your brother,
carefree with a future,
at one, with one another.

No, your riches live within you,
hidden deep inside,
– your tenderness, and sweet caress,
that kept her satisfied.

If you're wondering
about this note,
she'd never thought to write,
she needs to say what's in her heart,
(before she falls apart).

She wouldn't want to own you,
hurt or say goodbye,
you're all to her, her one desire

– until the day she dies..

Shallow

Love, when lost,
– a mystery,
arrived, then disappeared,
a love so deep and tender,
for only one of you
– it seems.

It came and went,
without a reason why,
left her devastated,
in despair without a care.

Her days are dark,
her nights more so,
dawn is just a shadow,
a veil that mystifies her love,
for him,
whose love was shallow.

One day, her dawn
will face the sun,
its light dispense the shadows,
– and him,
who drifted from her life,
the cause of all her sorrow.

Mistaken

She won't beg, or plead, or cry,
without him by her side,
but he must know,
before too late,
how she felt inside.

Was she so deluded,
imagined far too much,
enfolded in his arms that day
– felt his tender touch?

Was he a dark deceiver,
a chancer on the make,
saw her as a loser,
or just a big mistake?

She understood the real man,
his voice gave him away,
it spoke and sang of love and loss,
in songs of yesterday.

Their ending was so brutal, tho',
no sorry or goodbye,
– left her in the wilderness,
left her wondering why.

He's not to blame
for how she felt,
– the passion was all hers,
she should have known,
right from the start,
another woman
shared his heart.

Endings are beginnings,
mistakes are in the past,
tomorrow dawns a future
where love and hope may last.

She kept a precious token, tho'
from him she found, then lost,
his voice remains – a gift he gave,
– his songs of love and loss.

Encounter

Each day we pass a stranger,
say hello, or not, who cares?
but one day in a million,
your "someone" may appear.

Chance is round a corner,
an encounter, nonetheless,
mystery, its master,
coincidence – perhaps?

It's when the fates come calling,
when we're unprepared
that Destiny and all her stars,
will find us unawares.

Will you encounter love one day,
or hate beyond expression,
or a sadness that will break you
from a stranger's indiscretion?

One chance encounter, stuff of dreams,
a meeting of two minds,
is when the gods anoint us
with a love that's rarely found.

Hers was when her firstborn cried,
a gift that came from Heaven,
when she arrived, a stranger,
the "one" she'd love forever.

Chance, you see, had caught her,
when she found herself with child,
encountered life's great mystery,
held fast by her, inside.

Mystery had mastered her,
when she became a mother,
encountering divinity,
destined for each other.

Power

One man,
a lone deceiver,
one man,
a lone dictator,
one man is all it takes,
one man,
a nation's leader.

One man who steals the souls of sons,
sends them into battle,
obeys his wish to demonise,
destroy the planet's masses.

One man alone, a heart of stone,
commands a reign of terror,
strikes without compassion,
– power is his pleasure.

One man with evil in his sights,
one mission to complete,
ruler of the darkness,
– but one that we'll defeat.

One woman though,
might make him see,
bring him to his knees,
herself upon a mission,
demanding his submission,
from the power of her written word,
bullets from her pen,
her weapon of destruction,
more powerful than him.

Before Too Late...

If you were lost tomorrow,
– gone for all of time,
would she regret not telling you,
all that's on her mind?

But you're still here
and so is she,
time enough to say,
her love for you is endless,
– forever and a day.

You have to know
– before too late,
what you have meant to her,
who loved you with a passion
she can hardly bear.

She knows you'll never feel the same,
(but that's another story),
true love will always pay the price,
– her dues were paid,
you were her life.

You'll always be " the one"
– she said so, many times,
you laughed
as though a madness
had confused a simple mind.

Madness maybe, but the bliss,
of being by your side,
alone, at one, togetherness,
with love she couldn't hide.

So now you know
just how she feels,
– not left it all unsaid,
you'll always be her only one,
the "one" she can't forget.

Three Little Words...

She tried to write
three little words,
perhaps he'll never hear,
because to her,
they're precious,
can't be wasted – like her tears…

Three little words, unspoken,
whispers on the wind,
awakened from a longing,
– the one that never ends.

Three little words
but power packed,
diamonds of the soul,
glittering with passion,
eternal as pure gold.

One day, her moment
came – then went,
drifted out of sight,
when he left her in the shadow
of an endless, cheerless, night.

Three little words of wonder,
was all she had to give,
(you know the kind
that says it all),
when spoken – with a kiss.

Three little words – so simple,
the only ones that matter,
too much, perhaps,
for him to hear,
– too much, it seems,
for her to bear.

Dust

Just listen to the lowlife
mindless imbeciles,
war lords of the universe,
– with evil on their minds.

They rise amongst the innocent,
intent on persecution,
maniacal, demonic,
with a thirst for insurrection.

"Get thee behind me Satan"
is a phrase that comes to mind,
meaning on your way my friend,
it's time to say goodbye.

Say goodbye to all your flawed designs,
(words that ill define), to a spirit
that controls your thoughts
and of your kindred kind.

Deceivers all, that come to life,
residing in the dark,
in the recess of a twisted heart,
devoid of any light.

All of us, the ones who share,
our love, compassion, – need to care,
the great, the good, the sisterhood,
man, in all his glory,
suffer in the silence
of a planet in despair.

We, you see, will overcome
be your master, understand ?
you have the time, you must decide
to change, be one of us,
learn to love,
not hate, my friend,

– before you turn to dust.

Apart

Wasted hours,
wasted days,
wasted hopes,
wasted dreams.

All of which
have come to pass,
when you and her
were meant to last.

Hours.
Days.
Long lonely nights,
– for her alone,
a broken heart.

Broken, lost,
apart from you,
her life has
lost all meaning,
but life's too short to waste on love,

– if love is only dreaming….

Broken

Her days grew dark,
her nights were cold,
when love was thrown away,
she wandered through the ether,
a soul that lost its way.

Heal her heart, why don't you?
it's broken and won't mend,
aching with a tenderness,
a pain that never ends.

It sighs and moans
for your embrace,
for you and her together,
wordless with the wonder
of loving one another.

Perhaps you'll call
one day or night,
speak your truth
put wrongs to right.

She'll wait, because,
she trusts in you,
the essence of your being,
the man, the boy, the whole of him,
body, soul,
skin to skin.

Truce

If this is war between us two,
– if so,
let's call a truce,
peace and love
mean more to me,
perhaps you feel that too?

One word from you, if you'll agree
would be enough – like "how are you",
or better still, three little words
to say,
I – do – love – you.

Yesterday has come and gone,
endings are beginnings,
tomorrow holds a promise
– with both our faults forgiven….

Silence

Listen, listen to the silence,
the silence of a mind,
devoid of all the messages
conducting us through time.

Messages from moments,
invasions that won't cease,
clicks and whistles, rowdy songs,
demolishing the peace.

Peace, the gift of silence,
a void where we might find,
a purity of spirit,
in the heartlands of the mind.

Can you hear the whispers,
the clamour in your head,
emanations of a thought form
desperate to exist?

In a war of words unspoken,
with a truth that cannot wait,
a truth that may annihilate
cause havoc in its wake.

So, listen to the silence,
be still and feel the vibe,
be free from
wordy warfare,
to find your peace of mind.

Chancer

A smooth sophistication,
a wry and subtle smile,
tactics of a player,
a deceiver in disguise.

No loving words were spoken,
no promises were made,
though mesmerised, adoring,
he left her in the shade.

Aloof, detached, a charmer,
practised in his art,
he came, then left,
without her,
– tore her world apart.

He slipped into the ether,
his hunting ground of choice,
searching for another prey,
feeling no remorse.

His modus operandi
served him well,
– until he met,
another willing woman,
– one he won't forget.

This one loved him, really did,
discovered his true self,
the man, the boy, the lover,
broken, like herself.

With time and love to nurture,
she hoped to heal his heart,
expose his alter ego,
turn his darkness into light.

Show how to love a woman,
with tenderness and trust,
emotion and devotion,
but most of all, with truth.

This story has no ending,
a tale, as old as time,
her love for him,
still growing,
tho' she can't help
wondering why.

Today

Today is mine,
– not yours,
because,
your page is blank,
obscure,
awaiting for the written word,
words to speak
my all.

Today is mine,
an open door,
my script is open ended,
– one page, alone,
unwritten,
the one where you're
forgiven.

Today is mine,
an open door,
– hope is on the handle,
the lock just needs the key
you lost,
the one that you abandoned.

Share my day, why don't you?
shelter in my heart,
don't make the final chapter
the one where we must part.

In all your days
– and all your nights,
will you think of me?
a woman of her word, who wrote,
with words of love
– her words of hope.

Distracted

She sits and wonders, what
or if,
or why
or when, or how?
– meandering her reasoning
with thoughts in overdrive.

She settles on a notion
– from where she cannot say,
tries to understand a world,
where evil stalks its prey.

Flitting through such messages
from media and press,
she hopes to make some sense of all,
the nations in a mess.

– But then she is distracted
by beauty she can see,
in a garden that is blooming
with scent and honey bees.

Peace will overcome her,
ease the panic in her head,
when seeds of love she planted,
will grace her flower bed.

Each seed contains a promise,
a shell of hidden depths,
a gift we take for granted,
tho' thankful nonetheless.

Her mind and mood will come to rest,
all worries left behind,
when she ponders on the miracle
of life below the ground.

Torn

She never knew – until they met,
her soul was incomplete,
one half was hers,
the other his,
but did he care? She thought he did.

Too late for her, perhaps for him,
their moment in the sun,
that came and went in shadow,
– in a heartbeat he was gone.

Torn in two, she watched him go,
her soul would follow him,
– his was still a part of her,
if they should meet again.

We journey through the aeons,
to brave those stormy seas,
where fate and all her wonders,
designed our destinies.

Destiny denied her though,
his love was lost to her,
fate and all her wonders
had left her in despair.

Adrift

In tidal waves of longing,
she's adrift on open seas,
drowning in an ocean,
from the deluge of her tears.

All she sees inside her head,
the landscape of her dreams,
are visions of
what might have been,
with him, she was complete.

"If only",
is her mantra,
beseeching in despair,
pleading to the heavens
languishing in prayer.

Love is
timeless tenderness,
true, but with a twist,
once given there's
no turning back,
a soul is sold
– with just one kiss.

Too much for her,
and him – maybe,
to ride the stormy seas,
of life with all its bittersweet,
adrift in shattered dreams.

Light

We speak of light, but do you see
the light of love, the inner me?

You are that light,
I shared its power with you,
alight with love
– I thought we could,
live in ecstasy.

The light became a rainbow,
a bridge of many colours,
a stepping stone, a fantasy,
where you and I were lovers.

My rainbow faded one dark day,
lost its power and might,
lost in clouds without the sun,
giver of the light.

Your light is still within me tho',
a portal in the dark,
residing in the valleys,
of my sad, pulsating heart.

We speak of light,but will you see,
the light of love – the inner me?

Perfection

Should I care about the wrinkles
that pucker up my skin,
or worry exponentially
about my double chin?
– or judge my daily happiness
compared to someone else,
someone who seems perfect,
nothing like myself?

So what is more acceptable,
beauty or the mind,
a nature that is loveable,
or a perfect, pert behind?

Who will love a feisty woman?
– a woman just like me,
some would say a diva,
with a soul no one can see!

Her love comes with a passion,
selective, that is true,
in you she found perfection
– but was she
good enough for you?

Summer

All her days were summer
when you were by her side,
no winter skies, or stormy clouds
could veil the love,
she tried to hide.

Before, in time, before you met,
before, when time stood still,
her heartlands were a wilderness,
a desert without you.

Summer, then, was endless,
day and night all one,
the wilderness had flowered,
life had just begun.

Too soon her summer faded,
like you, it lost its light,
day became a torment
longing for the night.

Night, where you descended,
invading every dream,
a desert of delusion,
haunts her, once again.

Wonder

Wonder, a mighty gift,
a talent sometimes lost,
in the hustle and the bustle,
of a nation in a rush.

No time to stop,
no time to kill.
Got to go,
can't stand still!

Fill the moment,
what to do?
Work and sleep,
wake, then go!

Slaves to time,
no time to care,
to wonder what,
or why or where.

Day to night will come and go,
without a second look,
at the wonder of a planet,
spinning like a top.

Hurling through the heavens,
a global entity,
hosting all humanity,
cruising through one day.

Passing through a starlit sky,
the moon will nod hello,
the sun will cast a blessing,
– teach the plants just how to grow.

The wonder of a rain soaked sky,
brings the living waters,
gives succour to the seeds of life,
– without its gift
we can't survive.

So when you have a moment,
wonder, take your time,
wonder at the universe,
a miracle – divine.

Imagine

Imagine if the sky fell in,
the stars forgot to shine,
the seas rolled back against the tide,
the moon was lost to time.

Imagine if no one was there
to hold you in their arms,
cocooned in perfect harmony,
underneath the stars.

Imagine that my love would last,
in tempest and in tears,
survive the bitter cold of loss
when hope had disappeared.

Imagine if my love for you
was all you ever wanted,
that life with you,
my everything,
was happy ever after.

Imagining, a madness of the mind,
where nothing is reality,
a place to waste our time,
to lose all sense
of self – unless,
your thoughts
were just like mine.

Spectre

Loving him was just too much,
she wasted from the wanting,
senseless in the suffering,
consumed in deep emotion.

She should have known,
– but didn't care
– all she saw was
him,
an image of perfection,
but one that disappeared,
faded as a shadow,
that hides itself from sun,
who left without a word to say,
goodbye,
– then he was gone.

Had she invoked a spectre,
created from a dream?
he, who came to comfort
but wasn't what he seemed.

Soul

She saw inside your soul that day,
(but you were blind to hers),
the music of your mind was all,
she'd ever want to hear.

It spoke to her without a voice ,
no need for conversation,
all of you lived in her head,
fused, entwined,
with nothing said.

The rhythm of
your heartbeat,
would pound
inside her soul,
the one you
never noticed,
the one that
says she's yours.

A symphony is playing,
a rhapsody in song,
the one where you incarnate,
with her,
where you belong.

Lifetime

Forever was a lifetime
while she waited just for you,
perhaps too late,
some might say,
tho' love will
always find a way.

You overwhelmed her with the bliss,
– a fierce and searing tenderness.

Never, ever, will it die,
for you're her only true desire.

She'll never know if you loved her,
– your passions lay elsewhere,
but the agony of losing you,
is more than she can bear.

Today is just another day,
to pass, without you there,
another day,
– like all the rest,
a vacant void
of emptiness.

Ignited

The passion that she feels for you,
is with her night and day,
deep within, she can't explain,
the ache, the pain,
what might have been.

You're in her every moment,
awake, asleep, existing,
as though you live within her soul,
the altar of her being.

Each day for her is torment,
each day a sunless sky,
though heaven could be
yours and hers,
wandering the stars.

Your star and hers together,
twin galaxies of light,
powered by emotion,
– when you and her ignite.

Unleashed

Loving him without due care,
(the only gift she had),
her heart and soul
would merge with his,
never holding back.

Chance, you see,
or fate maybe,
(some would say her destiny),
arrived without a warning,
took her to the edge and back,
dissolved her with the wanting,

A powerhouse of passion
alone unleashed for him,
long buried, long forgotten,
for her, a mortal sin.

Her soul took flight, reached the heights,
revealed a hidden depth,
with him she found herself again,
reborn, renewed,
possessed.

Happiness

Where is your greatest happiness,
who is your everything,
what is it that you're longing for,
awakes your soul to sing?

Is it in a hoard of gold,
a fast expensive car,
or beauty and perfection
– or someone to adore ?

Will you find it in the mirror,
see a truth in your reflection,
a life well lived, untainted,
or a heart that's ever breaking?

Happiness is all we crave,
waiting, always wanting,
for peace and love, in harmony,
the wonder of our being.

Of being in the moment,
casting off despair,
savouring each other,
knowing someone cares.

When happiness is tested,
when hope has disappeared,
when life with all its torment,
is when we feel the fear.

Fear of desolation,
fear of losing love,
fear of what the future holds
– but most of all,
– of loss.

Remember though, that
nothing lasts,
like storm clouds,
all will pass,
happiness is hope reborn,
where sadness is
– dismissed.

A Fairy Tale

Do you believe in fairy tales?
she did – her first mistake;
Prince Charming was a player,
a roguish reprobate.

He made the moves, threw a her line,
(you know the type I mean),
he cast his net, caught his catch,
then gently reeled her in.

He said she was a genius,
clever at her craft,
praised her with such eloquence,
said she was first class.

She saw him as her Superman,
perfect in her sight,
gentle, smooth, well practised,
he took her by surprise.

Together, they became as one,
in secret rendezvous,
closer than she could believe,
all her dreams come true.

The songs he sent that spoke of love,
passionate with longing,
were those he heard long years ago,
love songs, full of yearning.

Played them when he called on her
– at the dead of night,
spoke to her of family,
the journey of his life.

She learnt to love, to trust in him,
his kind and gentle manner,
was all she could have wanted,
– but Superman – he wasn't.

Was it a front, a mask he wore?
before he walked away;
no midnight calls or visits,
nor even goodbye kisses.

No calls to say or reason why,
gone to God knows where,
he melted like a shadow,
without a moment's care.

Her days were dark, her nights were cold,
life had slipped away,
bewildered in a twilight,
her soul had lost its way.

She wants him in her arms tonight,
tomorrow is too late,
she'll worship and adore him
– unless he hesitates.

Our woman will be waiting,
her door still open wide,
a gateway to a state of bliss,
their path to Paradise.

Abandoned then, forsaken,
she locked her heart to love,
closeted herself away,
spurned,
Miss Understood.

Why can't he heal her broken heart?
the one he needs to mend,
that's aching with such tenderness,
a pain that never ends.

She sighs and moans for his embrace,
his soul and hers together,
wordless with the wonder,
of loving one another.

Perhaps he'll call one day or night,
speak his truth
before too late,

– before the end of time.

Once...

Once,
when he was new to her
and she was new to him,
when life was still serene to her,
he changed her destiny.

Changed her in a moment
from the woman she once was,
felt the gift of his caress,
melted from his tenderness.

Who knew that in one moment,
burning with a fire,
her world would change forever,
abandoned to desire?

She should have known
they couldn't last,
but blinded with a passion,
she didn't see the parting
Destiny was planning.

Once again, she found herself
without her someone special,
the one that gave her meaning,
– the one who left her grieving.

Left her in a wilderness,
the hollows of her mind,
where she was just surviving,
tho' dying deep inside.

Once, she was elated,
with him she was complete,
but then her life had ceased to be
denied and in defeat.

A darkness had descended,
felt her life
had all but ended,
as day and night
remained the same
when all she did
was call his name.

Living but not loving,
her light had dimmed,
switched off,
won't reappear – until he's there,
holding out his hand…

Love is such a mystery,
– emotion is surreal,
suffusing all our senses,
enfolding us in dreams.

Empty

Today is just another day,
empty without you,
tomorrow will be just the same
– unless you say hello.

So much to share,
if you should dare,
like all our yesterdays,
when we were in
each other's arms,
just us, without a care.

Tempest

There's a raging tempest,
a storm that won't subside,
in the portals of her heartstrings,
in the heartlands of her mind,
invading all her senses,
in each and every moment,
controlling all emotions,
the ones that left her broken,
the ones that had infused her
with an all consuming fire,
the kind that man and woman
want and most desire.

The ones that will define them
in the journey of their lives,
searching for their only one,
their guide to Paradise.

Paradise,
the home of bliss,
for most is hard to find,
but when they met one perfect day,
she found it in his eyes,
found it without searching
when fate had cast her spell,
– tho' when that spell was broken,
her heaven turned to hell.

There's a raging tempest,
a storm that won't subside,
a storm that won't extinguish
– the fire in her heart.

The Wait

As a woman of a certain age, she'd
gained that certain look,
with wrinkled skin, and double chins –
in total body shock!

What to do? Forget it!
The rot had gone too far;
all the creams in fancy jars,
won't cure all that for sure.

So who would want a woman, diminished, ageing fast,
(her heart forever beating though),
if love should come to pass?

Her passions had remained the same,
heightened, she would say,
since when she had experienced,
much love that came her way.

Love for him she married,
(and the one or two before),
love for both her children,
and her dog that she adored!

Love had come in all its forms,
some left her with deep scars,
the good, the bad, it's fair to say,
from those that didn't care.
A rainbow of emotions – from hot to,
well, lukewarm,
her love life and its journey
is the story of us all.

She'd turned her back on thoughts she'd had,
of love and empathy,
quietly abandoning
herself to chastity.

Love did come, it found her,
left her breathless in its wake,
with him she found her reason,
– but had they
left it far too late?

Too late, maybe, for him,
– not her,
a case of wait and see,
still time enough to know for sure,
if he's the one – her true amour.

Affinity

Is there a truth in suffering,
a message for this life,
a meaning and a reasoning,
leading us to light?

Are there mentors that may guide us
– angels we can't see,
angels in a universe,
one for all of us,
– and me?

If that is so, I hope they'll hear
the cries of those forlorn,
abandoned to the depths of hell,
in wars and the unknown.

In killing fields between mankind,
in nations torn apart,
that lie upon the altars
of their mothers' broken hearts.

Torn and ravished innocents,
sacrificial lambs,
victims of a demon,
to die at his command.

There is a truth in suffering,
it's in your hands and mine,
say no to those that would destroy
the peace of humankind.

Make love not war,
that is to say,
love your fellow man,
feel the revelation,
of all that love can bring.

It's our only weapon
in a war of desecration,
all of us empowered
the answer and solution,
when just one man of evil,
dictates your fate and mine,
his citadel of hate my friend,
will crash, be cast aside.

Game

Love is all and everything,
nothing can compare,
it comes without a warning
or a sign to say, beware,
– if one day,
all the magic,
should melt and disappear.

Where does it go, I wonder,
back from where it came, or, linger in the shadows,
hunting for new game?

A game, perhaps, of hide and seek,
stalking for its prey,
ready with love's arrow
for those who lost their way,
– to pierce, inflict, the pain of love,
that none of us escape,
tho' everyone is willing
in a game,
of give and take.

The givers and the takers
will some day find "the one",
some will give too much, I fear,
the others, hit and run.

Love and chance go hand in hand,
blind to one another,
the test of time alone will find,
– if love will last for ever.

Eternal

He awakened her to passion,
she thought she'd locked away,
safe from all the pain and dross,
 – afraid to be betrayed.

He left her though, with memories,
sad songs with tender melodies,

 – his haunting last mementoes,
that taunt her in her sorrows.

Her senses are dissolving,
fading fast, she's lost her way,
searching for some solace
through a dark and endless day.

She's searching for a secret,
secreted in his soul,
in the recess of his being,
that left her in the cold.

Cold – but never doubting
that one day they will be,
eternally united,
should he return – for me...

Eternal,
 – an inferno
of passion on the loose,
is a fatal fascination
most of us would choose,
 – but,
should it die,
the embers will remain,
reminders of
our greatest love,
Eternal,
is its name.

Carousel

Round and round,
up and down,
a carousel in time,
Earth and all her passengers
transporting humankind.

The carousel will circle,
with everyone on board,
each on their own mission,
decreed by overlords.

In truth, we have free spirit
if the carousel should stop,
permitting all its passengers,
the chance to be dropped off.

Off into another realm,
free from bigotry,
oppression and disharmony,
find love, the Master Key.

The carousel's still moving,
the travellers are long gone,
gone to fate and fortune
– to find where they belong.
Are you
a lonesome traveller,
passing precious time,
astride upon a carousel,
going round and round?

Or, are you on the up,
not down,
forever optimistic,
spinning in the cosmos
deciding on your options?

Life's carousel will come to rest,
its mission quite complete,
awaiting for more passengers,
more souls in search of fate.

Too Late

You came,
you left,
but oh the in-between,
was glorious, just magical,
living in the dream…

For once I had allowed myself
to be the real me,
just for you, you understand,
no one else will do.

For me, you were perfection,
body, soul and mind,
a doorway into heaven,
– if you were by my side.

Owning you was not my thing,
– nor a wedding ring,
nothing more than you alone,
my love, my everything.

All I wanted was the truth,
that made you walk away,
left me in the abyss,
alone in purgatory.

I've closed the door to sweet amour
the one I shared with you,
too late, I think,
my sell by date,
is more than overdue…

But loving you
(the heartbreak too),
the yearning and beyond,
made me more a woman,
than you could ever know…

Wasteland

Trapped inside a wasteland,
a grey and empty void,
tormented with emotion,
I'm longing for your voice.

A longing that won't disappear,
won't leave until you come,
to take me in your arms again,
where you and I belong.

That day you held me in your arms,
safe and satisfied,
the world about me disappeared,
– I'd found my Paradise.

I feel you close around me,
your heartstrings next to mine
your fingertips caressing me,

– just a distant memory...

A memory I can't forget,
it stalks inside my head,
a vision with me night and day,
of loving you
– with no regrets.

Regret is for mistakes we make,
but you were no mistake,
your eyes met mine, a mirror
of two souls, who met
– too late...

If...

If both of you had met before,
when you were twenty-three,
would you have recognised yourselves,
reaching fifty-three?

– Or even in the after years,
lucky to survive,
all that life
had thrown at you,
– the journey of your lives.

Our souls have many pathways,
we stumble through them all,
oblivious and innocent
to what the future holds.

From night to day,
we make our way,
until, one day we find,
just what our hearts
were searching for,
– did someone yearn for yours?

Hope hovers in the shadows,
where love is safely hidden,
waiting for the moment,
for love to reawaken.

Love tho' never ages,
won't judge or die away,
it only sees perfection,
in the light of yesterday.

Time enough, no matter what,
for love to find a way,
be blind to imperfection,
in the sunset of our days.

Words

Of all the words she wants to say,
they're, "let me love you,
won't you stay?"

Words revolving round her head,
lamenting you with nothing said.

Words, emotions, disillusion,
for love that died
with no solution.

Questions, answers,
maybe lies?
all that's left
when dreams have died.

You were to her the morning star,
the dawning of a sunrise,
but sunset cast it shadow
when she gazed into your eyes.

Those eyes that spoke a thousand words,
words you left unsaid,
the only ones she wants to hear,
revolving round her head.

Locked

Remember, why don't you?
each moment you shared,
locked both together
devoid of all care.

Safe and secluded
with her in your arms,
– but never forever,
when you broke her heart.

Locked in and locked out,
she cannot escape,
tormented without you,
alone, locked away.

Away far away, dreaming of you,
locked in her heart,
forever apart.

Possessed

She's dying inside, cannot survive,
the longing, the aching,
destroying her mind.

What did you do? Why should she care?
You're only one man – there's plenty out there.

You've taken her over, possessed her sad soul,
the one that she gave
– that you left in the cold.

Safe in your arms, eternally yours,
all of her melted, but you never noticed.

She's dying inside, lost in a cloud
of endless devotion, where you are her world.

One day she'll recover – not now, it's too early,
her time tho' is slipping,
and yours may be fading.

"Make hay while the sun shines"
someone sane,
someone said,
take hold of your heart,
make it sing,
learn to live.

Loving is easy – just as before,
when you two
were lovers,
but now are no more.

Found

There is a place called Heaven,
she found it in your arms,
she found it in the breath you breathe,
she found it in your eyes.

She found it without searching,
she found that she could break,
she found that love's a sickness,
– she found out much too late.

Broken in two pieces,
one half is what you see,
the other is the essence
of what she used to be.

If Heaven is a healer,
why does her soul still weep?
tears that won't stop falling
for you to bring her peace.

Peace to overcome the pain,
the pain of losing you,
peace and sweet tranquillity,
– she only found with you...

Flight

Dissolving into nothing, a whisper on the wind,
afloat beyond the mist of time,
her soul had found its wings.

I sensed her passing moment,
free at last to be,
shared her flight,into the night,
to greet eternity.

I felt her smile,as though she said,
"I'm whole again, I've gone to rest,
to leave all care behind,
but you and I will meet again,
to dance among the stars".

From a mother to her daughter,
her lasting legacy,
a promise of togetherness,
of love, from her
– to me.

Reborn

As different as the sun and moon,
as night is from the day,
– until you found each other
then found you were the same.

You met in both your
day of day of days,
while you were still apart, knowing
– yet oblivious,
from aeons in the dark.

The dance began, you were to her,
the morning star she'd waited for,
enfolded in an aura,
of your soul, to be reborn,
– exploding in a symphony,
consumed within the bliss,
mind to mind,
renewed in time,
with love that
– couldn't last.

Moonlight

Meet me in the moonlight,
underneath the stars,
haunt me with the wonder
of the starlight in your eyes.

It's where your soul
and mine will meet,
to search each other's secrets,
of mystery and memory
of lovers and deceivers.

Mysteries and memories,
traces from the past,
clouds that bar a future,
when new love
may come to pass.

They're long gone,
but fate decreed
that we should be as one,
dancing in the moonlight,
where you and I belong.

I hear your voice,
I see your soul,
I gaze upon the moon,
wishing on a moonlit night,
for you to be my own.

So,
meet me in the moonlight,
underneath the stars,
make a wish,
come back to me,
take me in your arms.

One Word...

One word, was all it took,
one word, to change her world,
one day, one man, – herself, it seems
with just one word, destroyed a dream.

Was it "hello" – a subtle invitation,
a doorway into heaven
– or, "goodbye",
that left her grieving?

One word, the first,
that gave her hope,
his last, too much to bear,
– the first so full of promise,
but goodbye was all she heard.

It only took a moment
for them to say goodbye,
for her it was a lifetime,
of love,
that passed her by.

Surrender

Surrender, why don't you?
give into your dreams,
enfold your emotions,
awake to your needs,
– of love and devotion,
twin souls of the deep,
living within you,
– safe but asleep.

Asleep to the wonders
safely secluded,
until you awaken,
free from illusion.

Surrender why don't you?
find her – she's here,
waiting to hold you,
with nothing to fear.

Elusive

Elusive in spirit, parted from you,
she's formless, a shadow,
an echo of you.

Where are you?
she needs you, close to her heart,
melting together,
be yours, if you want.

– But is she mistaken,
too trusting, believing,
that you were an angel that led her to heaven?

Heaven on earth, a mirage maybe,
that mirrored a dream,
of all that could be.

Mr Wonderful

Tick – Tock goes the clock,
her time is passing by,
although she never noticed
when she was mesmerised.

She saw what she imagined,
her man, behind a mask,
her perfect Mr. Wonderful,
(tho' wonder wouldn't last).

It took some time (her clock was slow),
to understand her man,
what happened, why, or who he was,
good – or underhand.

Her clock ticked on – her days grew long,
still, she wondered why,
he'd left without an answer,

– but left his mask behind.

Diamond

She can't forget, won't forget,
will never, ever lose,
all the love she felt for you,
for love is what she chose.

She can love you from afar,
– or wish upon a star,
hold you in a memory,
know that's where you are.

A memory that flickers
in a soulful picture book,
relaying and replaying,
the story of her love.

It's where she goes to find you,
her diamond in the rough,
its light a hidden secret,
like yours,
– the one she loves.

Aura

They say that love is blind,
– it's true.
It surely was,
when she loved you.

She never saw it coming,
not wanting all the pain
only saw your spirit,
your heart and inner flame.

If love is like a thunderbolt,
lightning from the stars,
then loss is when your world caves in,
swallows up your heart.

Leaves a yawning chasm
from where there's no escape,
– the deep, that's all consuming,
a suffocating grief.

If love is blind, why does she see
an aura of perfection?
– your soul an emanation
to heal her desolation.

Love you see, is all there is,
without it, hope is void,
but with your love, you both can be,
the essence of pure joy.

Heat

Only him, there's no one else,
tho' ageing like herself,
although she'd never notice,
all she wanted was himself.

Powered by a passion,
ignited with a fever,
the heat of him possessed her then,
she'd found her inner diva.

He'd felt himself reborn, he said,
as though he was nineteen,
enraptured in the moment,
two players in a dream.

Her dreams became akin to clouds,
flotillas in blue skies,
passing through the heavens,
ethereal, divine.

Too soon those clouds
and dreams would fade,
dissolving in the ether,
beyond her reach, behind a veil,
of him,
she'd lost forever.

Miracle

Every day's a miracle – if you can see the sky,
if you can hear the birds sing,
or hear a newborn cry.

Every day's a miracle – if you can wonder why,
or take a breath and say hello,
to make that someone smile.

Every day's a miracle – if you can take a step,
make footprints in the sands of time,
just like the day we met.

Every day's a miracle – mine was when we shared,
a tenderness of spirit
a moment without a care.

Every day's a miracle – until that last goodbye,
when time decides it's time to go,
to leave for Paradise.

Tho' Paradise could still be yours,
it's not too late to be,
together in the miracle,
of here and now

– with me.

Drumbeat

Is there another word for Love?
tell me if you know,
could L be for the Longing,
or O for when it's Over,
or V for Veneration
or E for Endless yearning?

Four letters that may change your life,
written by a lover,
(better though when whispered,
with both of you together).

Set to music in a lullaby,
love is carried on a song,
from a mother to her firstborn,
where the breath of life began.

We hear it in the drumbeat
of the heart when overcome,
pounding from the passion,
when loving comes along.

The French would say,
"Toujours l'amour"
an echo of romance,
a sentiment that's all the same,
no matter where it's from.

There is no other word for love,
for love is universal,
wherever it is spoken,
it conveys a vast emotion.

Four single letters locked together,
power in one word,
simple, but eternal,
with a message for the world.

One Day, One Man...

One day,
one man,
one woman,
one life of love to share,
one of them would love too much,
the other wouldn't care.

But still the world kept turning,
round and round it went,
but when he left her
one dark day,
it stopped
then she was lost.

Imploding with emotion,
in the depths of her despair,
he haunted all her senses,
in the river of her tears.

With nothing left,
she's just a mess,
slipping far away,
existing in a memory,
defined

in one dark day...

Him

Why is it she connects to him,
just him – there's no-one else,
why does she feel his pain and loss,
– he hides and fights against?

Why only him, she wants to know,
what is it that she feels?
Is it because that him and her,
aren't one, not two, but,
WE?

She knows what makes his soul vibrate,
what makes him want to weep,
what makes his soul to soar above,
to find his inner peace.

She knows without the telling
because he's part of her,
it's where she keeps him hidden,
in her heart,
that she laid bare.

Consumed

She loved him too much, possessed by his touch,
possessed with a madness
for all she had lost.

All of her wasted,
haunted with craving,
diminished in sorrow
becoming a shadow.

Could this be a woman
once proud and decisive,
wanting for nothing,
contented without him?

But love had consumed her,
buried her pride,
opened her heart,
brought her alive.

Loving too much would tear her apart,
without him she faded,
alone,
in the dark.

Boxed

She lives with little boxes,
inside is someone's heart,
saved from someone special,
– a gift that left its mark.

Some boxes are much bigger,
some are not so large,
all of them, tho' hold the keys
to someone else's heart.

Some boxes are festooned with gold,
glittering with stardust;
they're the ones she holds most dear,
– from love that was too much to bear.

The smaller ones are tucked away,
stacked upon each other,
they're the ones where hope was lost,
waiting for another….

One day – just when, who knows?
but then,
one box may just be opened,
to find inside, that love survived,
– inside a box, she'd set aside.

Icon

Skin to skin – awakening,
wanton with desire,
worshipping, adoring him
as tho' he was divine.

An icon of perfection
that only she would see,
until the Fates came calling,
said he wasn't what he seemed.

It's when she would awake – once more,
to leave her dreams behind,
his mask had slipped, revealed to her,
his masquerade, was just a game,
a player in disguise.

In dreamlands of the senses,
creations of the mind,
is where we mask reality,

for love is truly – blind.

So Near...

So near, so far, as tho' you are,
asleep inside her heart,
asleep, unless your dreams become,
entwined, to share with hers.

It's where she goes to find you,
in moments of despair,
when life without you by her side,
is more than she can bear.

Once, when you were strangers,
before she was aware,
before her heart was broken,
was when she didn't care.

But one fine day
all that would change,
loving you – a torment,
enamoured and adoring,
– then abandoned, without warning.

So near, so far, is where you are,
deep, within her heart,
where you're asleep, but where she keeps,
her dreams – that fell apart.

Portal

Can't see it, but you'll feel it
in the sanctity of soul,
delivered to the senses
heals the broken, makes them whole.

Its tenderness will open up
a portal where you'll find,
an answer to a prayer or two,
to soothe a troubled mind.

A mind like yours
that's searching for,
the one thing we all crave,
from when we were created
– until the end of days.

The one thing that
will shake the world,
bring evil to its knees,
the one thing that's eternal,
is all that mankind needs.

It comes in one big package
– a gift we can't refuse,
from one who makes your heartstrings
sing,
– your one and only, everything.

So what is "it"?

Don't ask me why,
you know, and so do I,
that love – in all its purest form,
– will lead to Paradise.

Ravaged

I'm wounded by the longing,
drowning in distress,
deep inside from where I hide
from love I can't forget.

I'm ravaged, torn in two,
blighted from the bliss,
seared, forever burning
in a cauldron of unrest.

Why was I so deluded
with an overwhelming passion,
knowing he had lost in love,
– from many indiscretions?

If I am just another,
a woman like the others,
why can't I see beyond the veil,
of truth he won't uncover?

The mystery, the one I feel
but cannot see,
shelters from beneath a mask
to shield himself from me.

Perhaps he doesn't know or care,
my love will always be
for him alone,
my life, my own,
my man of mystery.

Someone

You're her first thought
and her last,
her present
and her past.
She's someone who is searching for,
your soul, the inner you,
who senses your emotions
endured from long ago.

She understands your pain and loss
without an explanation,
wanting you to feel again,
the peace that only love can bring.

The passion and the pain of love,
go hand in hand, she knows,
perhaps one day
you'll meet again,
to find you were
twin souls.

That someone will be waiting,
until the end of time,
to share a new beginning,
for both of you to find,
that stairway in the stardust,
in the music from the gods,
in the wonder
of infinity
– in the sanctity of love.

Rhapsody

Hold me,
hold me one last time,
let me feel your heartbeat,
in rhapsody with mine.

Hold me fast, don't hold back,
let me be your all,
free me from
a world of pain,
hold me, love me,
once again.

Forever safe in your embrace
secluded in the silence,
the only place we're meant to be,
together in sweet harmony.

So hold me in your memory,
hold me in your heart,
save me in that special place,
the one where you ignite.

Honey Pot

Mankind is just a human hive,
busy like the bees,
tho' flightless individuals
– a honey pot of need.

Our queens of course
will rule the world,
give succour to man's cause,
birthing man as worker bees
or drones to fight in wars.

Buzzing in their element,
fighting for their lives,
worker bees remain resigned,
accepting their sad plight.

Scurrying and scavenging,
wanting to succeed,
workers in a frenzy
in money making schemes.

The hive tho' will contain them all,
reliant on the honey,
the sweetness will sustain them all
– the food of love
is what it's called,
attracting man and woman,
queen and drone alike,
in a honey pot of need you see,

– we're just the same as honey bees!

Raw

No one else would feel her pain,
an ache from losing love,
when all of her
would waste away
from passion turned to dust.

A holocaust inflamed her,
seared her soul away,
fading fast without him,
discarded and betrayed.

How could it be
that this one man
would haunt her all her days,
forever be a memory,
a dream of yesterday?

In days of raw emotion,
aching all alone,
all she would remember
was locked away, on hold.

Left alone, her fate was sealed,
his heart was hers forever,
bonded to her heartstrings,
safe, secure, protected.

Where are you?
she still wonders,
gazing at the stars,
heaving in the heartbreak,
longing for his arms.

This book is printed on paper from sustainable sources managed under the Forest Stewardship Council (FSC) scheme.

It has been printed in the UK to reduce transportation miles and their impact upon the environment.

For every new title that Troubador publishes, we plant a tree to offset CO_2, partnering with the More Trees scheme.

For more about how Troubador offsets its environmental impact, see www.troubador.co.uk/sustainability-and-community